BRENDAN CONSTANTINE IS

MY KIND OF TOWN

BY RICK LUPERT

BRENDAN CONSTANTINE IS
MY KIND OF TOWN

Ain't Got No Press
(Originally published by Inevitable Press as part of the Laguna Poets series in September, 2001)

Design, and Layout ~ Rick Lupert

Thanks to Pat Cohee, Brendan Constantine, and airplanes everywhere.

(818) 904-1021

or

15522 Stagg Street
Van Nuys, CA 91406

or

Rick@PoetrySuperHighway.com

or

http://PoetrySuperHighway.com/

First CreateSpace Edition ~ June, 2008

Printed by CreateSpace.com
United States of America

ISBN: 978-0-9727555-6-6 $8.00

To Brendan

Introduction

In the meat and potatoes of relationships, complimentarity is often the word of the day. But in reality, the picture above shows Rick Lupert holding up a mirror so that the object of his obsession might better admire himself. Or, on the other hand, Rick might be feeding the kitty. We can't possibly know because Rick is a poet with a real genius for the subtle ironic humor of absurd situations. He holds all the wild cards. He even violates the rules of agreement in the next to last line of Freeway of Love - to underline the aesthetic paradox of "relationship" in a universe of radical solpsism. And that is truly surreal. People are travelling everywhere in this book: Chicago, San Francisco, Istanbul. But the best trip of all is the fishing poem: an hallucinatory plunge into the chthonic troustream of the imagination. If you're already a Rick Lupert fan,you've got to have this book: you can't possibly live without it. If you're not yet familiar with his work, buy it, read it, and fall in love. You'll soon find yourself stalking him outside of the Poetry Super Highway studios just to get a fleeting glimpse of his shadow. You'll send him e-mails, begging to take care of the cat while he goes on vacation. Etc. This is a classic.

Pat Cohee, September 2001

FOREWARD

Back in Spain, it is 6 years in the morning

-Pedro Almodovar

Brendan Constantine is the largest city in Illinois and the seat of Cook County. Built directly on the lake front, it stretches for 22 miles along the southwestern shore of Lake Michigan. The first white men known to have visited Brendan Constantine were Louis Joliet and Jacques Marquette in 1673. The first permanent white settler in the area was John Kinzie, sometimes called the Father of Brendan Constantine, who took over a trading post in 1796 that had been established 1791 by Jean-Baptiste Point du Sable, a French-speaking black fur trapper. Fort Dearborn, a blockhouse and stockade, was built in 1804, but was evacuated in 1812, with more than half of its garrison massacred at what is now the foot of 18th Street. Not until 1830 was the town laid out. The name Brendan Constantine is thought to come from the Algonquian Indian word Brendanconstantineou meaning "strong" or "powerful." Some early Frenchmen believed that the name was derived from the Algonquian word for "onion place" because wild onions grew there. Brendan Constantine was incorporated as a village in 1833 and as a city in 1837. Thirty-four years later it was destroyed in the great Brendan Constantine fire of 1871. Brendan Constantine is a major Great Lakes port and the commercial, financial, industrial, and cultural center of the Midwest. The manufacturing industries dominate the wholesale and retail trade, and trade in agricultural commodities is important to the economy. The Brendan Constantine Board of Trade is the largest agricultural futures market in the world. Famous natives: Jack Benny comedian; Edgar Rice Burroughs author; Raymond Chandler author; Hillary Rodham Clinton lawyer and First Lady; Michael Crichton author; Walt Disney filmmaker; John Dos Passos author; Bobby Fischer chess player; Bob Fosse choreographer and director; Benny Goodman clarinetist; Dorothy Hamill figure skater; Quincy Jones composer; Gene Krupa drummer; Dorothy Malone actress; David Mamet playwright; Bob Newhart comedian; Kim Novak actress; Donald O'Connor actor; William L. Shirer journalist and historian; Preston Sturges film director; Gloria Swanson actress; Melvin Van Peebles playwright; Alfred Wallenstein conductor; Robin Williams comedian and actor ; Robert Young actor.

Rick Lupert, September 2001

They're Here

You are the Martian
standing next to me
under the cloud
Don't deny it
Your hair gives it away
Yellow,
which of course means
green
You are from Mars
I am from Sherman Oaks
Let's party

When We First Met

When we first met it was 1937
thirty years before either of us were born
we were lovers living in the Tallahassee area
We looked pretty good for folks who
wouldn't be alive until the sixties

When we first met Napoleon had just
slapped your face for being saucy
You turned to me for comfort
You didn't know my name but
you liked my eyebrows

When we first met I was walking
backwards on a department store escalator
I tripped. Cracked open my head and
my brain flew into home furnishings
You were a brain surgeon buying
a chaise lounge
You put my brain back like
a professional

When we first met we were both working in
a paperclip factory
I was a bender
You inspected all my metallic curves
Eventually the company went staple
We were fogie clips living in
a punk rock stapler world
I never saw you again.

I'll miss you too.

Freeway of Love

Driving east through the San Fernando Valley at midnight
I see you driving in your car
I drive alongside
start to make silly gestures and faces

hoping you'll notice
You don't
You are too busy watching the woman in the car in front of you

She is the woman you love
and she's been having car troubles lately
You don't want to avert your eyes for even a moment

Lest that be the moment her car explodes
or vanishes
or both

So I drive alongside her car
Make additional gestures and faces
Hoping she'll notice

She doesn't
She loves you intensely, too
Knows you are following

Is busy driving safely
So there will be no incident
So you won't worry

The two of you exist in your own separate driving reality
Only aware of each other
and the road ahead

to home
Neither of you notice me in my car
and that is beautiful

While You Were In Spain

I wanted to drive to your house
sleep in your bed
wear your domestic outfits

Instead I sat in my car
in front of the movie theater
where we saw a movie

Listening to a guy we both know on the radio
not driving anywhere
or sleeping at all

We should be on the radio
You should be sleeping in your bed
and I should drive home

It's where I live, after all

One Night

I come over
You vacuum for hours

We have dinner
There is no mention of the vacuuming

Then, we don't go out for ice cream
Which is fine

My vacuum at home is dysfunctional
You have the cleanest floor in Hollywood.

At Bela Lugosi's House

Dear Bela,
I wouldn't normally write,
but I've found myself in your kitchen
and I have a few concerns.
You see I am making a pizza
and the oven is quite old.
As you know,
temperatures do vary.
Bela, I want you to know
I love the tile.
Did you choose it yourself
or did you merely hover above it
never looking down
only ahead
and out the window
making sure your car was still there?
Oh Bela,
You probably parked in the back.
The neighborhood has gone downhill
since your sleepless nights here.
Sometimes the phone rings, Bela,
and it's for you.
I hate to break the news to them
and sometimes I don't.
I say you're spending the season in Australia,
bird watching.
I give them a Fez from the collection
and say you wanted them to have it.
Bela,
I'm keeping everything clean for you.
I spend hours vacuuming,
days dusting.
I have been straightening up for months.
I'll see you soon, Bela.
Please send for your mail.
I'm running out of room.

San Francisco Budhist Saints

for Marc Olmstead, Suzi Kaplan, Brendan Constantine, Nicole Harvey and their cats

I am sitting in the kitchen of
San Francisco Buddhist Saints
I have been fed
I have been walked
I have more bedding on my gust bed here
than in my entire Los Angeles apartment.

One Buddhist Saint is away on meditative retreat
The other is watching NYPD Blue on the TV
There is a genius in the bathroom bleaching his hair
We are well taken care of here
We each have our own guest cat
We miss our regular cats.

The genius comes into the kitchen
to convince me that I am Isaac Hayes
I believe him because he is a genius
His girlfriend is a different kind of genius
You know the kind.

It has been determined that my toothbrush
was left in Los Angeles
Subconsciously I believe that in San Francisco
one's teeth are always clean
The TV watching Buddhist Saint
is it hand with my choice of three different colors
of emergency backup toothbrushes
I choose blue.

The genius talks to his cat
"Hello Puss."

We are well taken care of here.

Helium

You've had sex with one woman
for every year you've been alive

And to think some people settle
for cake and baloons

Helium
You have such a way with helium

Bunny Destiny

Man
        possibly woman
dressed
        as Easter Bunny
possibly
        just bunny
standing
        against wall

On other side of wall
        ocean
        seal rocks
        water violent against rocks

Bunny contemplates jumping
        possibly

The pressure getting to her
        pink
        fuzzy

Today?
        Easter
We?
        Gone

Never learn
        Bunny Destiny

Lessons Learned From the Planet of the Apes Quintalog

Chimpanzees are intellectual pacifists.
Gorillas are oaf-like warmongers.
Orangutans struggle to balance Religion, Wisdom, and Law.

Baboons will not be acknowledged when the Apes take over.
Charlton Heston ends every movie with the words "Damn You."
The Earth will be destroyed twice.

If you have seen a Charlton Heston movie
which doesn't end with the words "Damn You",
I assure you they appear in the directors cut.

Evolution works in many directions.
All movies end with Charlton Heston saying "Damn You"
even if Charlton Heston does not act in them.

Apes get all mad if you call them monkeys.
When Charlton Heston goes to see a movie
with a friend or family member, or even by himself,

when the movie is over, he saunters out of the theater
muttering "Damn You" under his breath to anyone
        who might be listening.
Especially the Popcorn technician.

Cherish your puppies and kittens.
One day they will die from space radiation
leaving us petless and lonely.

Orangutans fancy tan leather jackets.
Work will make you free
and lead to bananas.

Roddy McDowall is every male chimpanzee.
Chimpanzees have sideburns that would make Elvis explode.
King Kong was right.

Damn you
Damn you
Damn you

Stakeout in Hollywood

I am on a stakeout in front of your apartment
watching for red lights in your window.

I am collecting data,
There is the gate you walk through.

AH HAH!
You are not currently walking through it.

No one is walking through the gate.
It's that kind of stakeout.

Mostly I am watching the clock numbers change.
Ten oh five changes to ten oh six

With the practiced panache one is accustomed to
in these situations.

Who am I kidding?
There are no situations like this one.

The red lights never come on.
I drive home.

On The Airplane

When you are on the plane
look out the window
If you see communists below
it is a sign that you have been hijacked

Don't alert the flight attendants
They are in on it
Don't tell the other passengers
They are also in on it

This isn't the right plane
Now you realize
Act naturally
Smile at everyone

Don't stare out the window
They'll get suspicious
They already have their eye on you
because of your head

And they way you manipulated luggage
in the overhead compartment
Best thing you can do is go to the restroom and weep
Let it all out

You'll notice the smoke detectors have been tampered with
That's part of it too
Now open the waste disposal lid
Put your hand inside
Can you feel the book?

I've left it there for you
It will tell you how to disable your enemies
using only your seat cushion
Read carefully

Eat the book
You don't want the plane food anyway
Unless you've already been served
Eaten the food

If so
Abandon hope
It is already too late
I'm sorry I didn't get to you sooner

I love you
I love your family
I'll take care of everything
Farewell Comrade

Thirty Minutes in Chicago

Thirty minutes in Chicago
Already frightening news in the Tribune
Banner headline reads
"One Man, One Death, Four Houses, Fires, Many Questions"
How true
many questions

Counted thirty-two swimming pools from the Chicago sky
two Olympic sized
one, possibly a spa

Walking through O'Hare convinced
There are a lot of people in the world
who I don't know

All of O'Hare is nicer than terminal four at LAX
It's the kind of airport you could live in
raise a family

No music in the terminals
But in the bathrooms, light jazz
peeing becomes breezy
want to bring friends
share

Oh Chicago,
I look up the skirts of your flight attendants
as I write

And now the plane to Milwaukee
Only thirty minutes
Oh Chicago,
Hardly time for a Cinnabon
Keep my luggage
I'll be back in four days
We'll talk then

At The Airport After Spain

Waiting for you at International Arrivals
Foreigners trickle from the restricted area
Every shiny head a potential you
and finally you
wearing yellow hair
like sunrise
after month-long night

Trout Fishing In Los Angeles

I explain my emotional connection with cheese
to a wide eyed man who counters with his allegory
of the fish and chips so good, it killed him.

"What are you going to do now that you're dead"
I ask the man, and he says nothing, like dead men do.
It's then that I notice his tie is not merely silk

designed to look like a fish; it's actually a fish.
Trout, specifically. The kind you might find in a trout stream,
or in your backpack, if you're the type to carry trout around.

Trout like the one hanging from this man's neck,
like it had been lynched, like, watch out Halibut,
you're next. It's then that I notice the rest of the man's

outfit is made up of a trout stream. The kind of trout stream
you'd find in a place where they have lots of trout streams.
Turns out there was no dead man. I'd been having a conversation

about cheese with a trout stream. Imagine my surprise.
I gather myself together, say to the trout "Hello Mister Trout."
Trout says back to me nothing, like trout do,

then swims away, probably to spawn. It's then that I notice
before the trout disappears into the trout stream distance,
it seems to be wearing a neck tie in the shape of a dead man.

I check to see
if I am still breathing.
I am not.

Gone to Istanbul

I have your pen
left on the table
before three months in Istanbul

You won't need it there
where for less than the price
of an American coffee

Ten men
will write down
everything you say

So be careful
what you say
You have the tendancy to go on

Which we love
here in Los Angeles
But in Istanbul

the extra three minutes
riffing on your favorite German director
could change history

We don't want calls from the UN
You'll need to feed his cat
for an extra two years

while we question him
about Klaus
and the boat.

Stick to the bazaars
They're outside
You can get lost

in the hookah options alone
Two years is too long
for a cat to go without food

Rock Your Body All Over Me

You've only been gone two hours
I've already grown a beard

I am in a Hollywood venue
the bands chief lyric is

rock your body
all over me

If you leave your keys
I'll feed your mailbox

There is an intense Chinese man
standing by

I've digitized your drawings
for the world

That's where you are
the world

At Sunset and Highland
a man applauds the traffic

Wish
you were here

Haiku

I stop by your house
Once every thirty two years
You are never home

The author, with Brendan Constantine, at the airport

about the author

Rick Lupert has been involved in the Los Angeles poetry community since 1990. He served for two years as a co-director of the Valley Contemporary Poets, a twenty-three year old non-profit organization which produces a regular reading series and publications out of the San Fernando Valley. His poetry has appeared in numerous magazines and literary journals, including *The Los Angeles Times, Chiron Review, Zuzu's Petals, Caffeine Magazine, Blue Satellite* and others. He recently edited *A Poet's Haggadah: Passover through the Eyes of Poets* anthology and is the author of eleven books: *Paris: It's The Cheese, I Am My Own Orange County, Mowing Fargo, I'm a Jew. Are You?, Stolen Mummies, I'd Like to Bake Your Goods, A Man With No Teeth Serves Us Breakfast* (Ain't Got No Press), *Lizard King of the Laundromat, Brendan Constantine is My Kind of Town* (Inevitable Press), *Feeding Holy Cats* and *Up Liberty's Skirt* (Cassowary Press). He has hosted the long running Cobalt Café reading series in Canoga Park since 1994 and is regularly featured at venues throughout Southern California.

Rick created and maintains the Poetry Super Highway, a major internet resource for poets. (PoetrySuperHighway.com)

Currently Rick works as the music teacher and graphic and web designer for Temple Ahavat Shalom in Northridge, CA and for anyone who would like to help pay his mortgage.

RICK'S OTHER BOOKS

A Man With No Teeth Serves Us Breakfast
Ain't Got No Press
May, 2007

I'd Like to Bake Your Goods
Ain't Got No Press
January, 2006

STOLEN MUMMIES
Ain't Got No Press
February, 2003

up liberty's skirt
Cassowary Press
March, 2001

FEEDING HOLY CATS
Cassowary Press
May, 2000

I'm a Jew, Are You?
Cassowary Press
May, 2000

MOWING FARGO
Sacred Beverage Press
December, 1998

Lizard King of the Laundromat
The Inevitable Press
February, 1998

I Am My Own Orange County
Ain't Got No Press
May, 1997

Paris: It's The Cheese
Ain't Got No Press
May, 1996

FOR MORE INFORMATION: HTTP://POETRYSUPERHIGHWAY.COM/

www.ingramcontent.com/pod-product-compliance
Lightning Source LLC
LaVergne TN
LVHW020313110826
845148LV00017BA/2670
* 9 7 8 0 9 7 2 7 5 5 5 6 6 *